LOCAL GHOSTS
True stories of odd happenings

compiled by
Margaret Royal and Ian Girvan

ABSON BOOKS · ABSON · WICK · BRISTOL

ABSON BOOKS Abson Wick Bristol England
First published August 1976
Second revised edition May 1984
Second impression April 1986
Third impression April 1990
Compiled by Margaret Royal and Ian Girvan
© Margaret Royal and Ian Girvan

Printed by Burleigh Press Ltd. Bristol BS2 0YA.
ISBN 0 902920 58 8

Introduction

This is our second revised edition of ghost stories. All are the result of original research and all, with the exception of one or two from Bath, are published for the first time.

For the second edition we have spread our net wider to take in much more of Avon and Somerset. Bristol ghosts are now thicker on the ground (or thinner in the air?) and places as far afield as Wedmore and Trowbridge are included.

We should like to thank our readers for sending us details of their experiences – one woman wrote from Canada describing a haunted night at the 'George and Pilgrim', Glastonbury – which we have included.

We hope that the following stories will pass a pleasant hour and give food for thought, however insubstantial.

Margaret Royal
Ian Girvan

The House of the Cursed Wind and Other Stories (*Bath/Bristol & environs*)

A rambling mansion in Kensington, Bath, is haunted by the ghost of a Lady Betty who many years ago fell in love with her groom. When the couple were caught fleeing the house by her father he flung her down the front steps and broke her neck.

Since that time several people have seen the figure of a grey lady in the house.

Every so often the house becomes very draughty, as if there were a gale blowing, even though there is no wind.

★   ★

Mr. Ronald B. Horstmann, of Merryfields, Colerne, wrote to tell us of a boyhood experience in Bath.

He relates, "We were a large family of seven living at No. 10 Widcombe Crescent with our two parents and my mother's step-mother (my step-grandmother) of whom we were all very fond.

"My grandmother was a wonderful old lady until she was over eighty but then she began to fail in health. She used to sit in a special armchair in the drawing-room above the dining-room. One day she fell from her chair with a great 'bump' which shook the chandelier in the dining-room where we were all having a meal.

"My mother ran upstairs to find my grandmother on the floor, very unwell after her fall, and she didn't survive for long. Periodically after her death, we heard the same sort of 'bump' upstairs and the chandeliers would rattle. The first two or three times we went upstairs to find out what had happened, only to find that all was in order.

"After a time we ignored this strange happening.

"When we had visitors they used to remark on the 'bump' and the rattling of the chandelier and we had to say it was nothing. This happened many times, usually, I seem to remember, at about the time that my grandmother had the fatal fall from her chair."

★   ★

A busy and mischievous ghost haunts the 'Waggon and Horses' at Peasedown St. John, run by Mr. Norman Harrison, on the Wells Road, some eight miles out of Bath.

It dislikes newcomers who stay the night at the pub and usually makes itself known at about two or three in the morning. Mr. Harrison's sister was one victim and was startled in the early

4

morning by the figure of a man in a black hat standing by the bed.

Mr. Harrison's parents had an umbrella thrown on to their bed and his mother had her face stroked.

A ball of string that he was using to line up ceiling tiles vanished for three months. He found it again when it was thrown at him in the pub's cellar. This was not the only incident. On another occasion he and a friend heard a lot of noise coming from the cellar. When he investigated he was bombarded with empty beer crates which were being thrown up the cellar steps.

The poltergeist has also swapped tools he and his brother-in-law were using to do a job in the house from one to the other.

The Harrison's are not frightened by their ghostly lodger but Mr. Harrison finds its habit of altering the pressure of the gas used for the beer rather trying. It also worries him when he has to go out.

★   ★

Mrs. Sally Pike of 14 St. John's Road, Warminster, reports that a cowled figure has been seen by several people at different times at this address. It haunts the hall and stairs. It stands quietly, face hidden, then slowly fades.

Both Mr. and Mrs. Pike, who have lived in the house for several years, have seen the figure. Mrs. Pike says there used to be a monastery nearby.

Mrs. Pike told Mrs. Royal that some friends were walking in the woods near Shearwater one day when they came across two fair-sized pools. They felt they were being watched from the trees on the other side of one of the pools and it made them feel uneasy.

When they walked round to the other side, they realised the 'watcher' had also changed sides. One of their friends took a picture across the pool which when it was developed and printed showed what appeared to be a strange figure rising out of the water.

It seemed to be covered in weeds and was wearing a pointed cap.

★   ★

For many years there has been a ghost in the Christopher Hotel, Bath. Miss Karen Lovell, the daughter of the hotel's owner, says she has experienced a very creepy feeling in one of the bedrooms and that other people have commented on the same thing.

Mrs. Royal, who has been in the room, says she had a feeling of being watched. It was a 'shivery sensation'.

People sleeping in the room have had their bed clothes tugged. The unseen presence seems not to like company. When the room was being redecorated it moved out into another part of the hotel and returned when the decorating had been completed.

Several guests have asked to be moved out of the room because they found the atmosphere too unnerving.

★   ★

A house in Caledonian Road, Bath, then occupied by a Mr. Richard Marchant, was plagued by a strange 'ticking' noise that started quietly before working up to a crescendo.

Mr. Marchant says that at one time the ticking stopped for several months. It then began again, this time behind the photo of his daughter, Nicola, on the sitting-room mantelpiece. When the photograph was touched, it stopped. Eventually it travelled all over the house but could be silenced at a touch.

Mr. Marchant also tells us that he was driving through Sharpstone, Freshford in Bath at 1.30 in the morning when he saw a white, cowled figure cross the road in front of him. It entered the front garden of a house called 'Wee House' and vanished. The front garden is open to the road and there is nowhere a person could hide. The owners of the house were friends of Mr. Marchant and knew nothing of the matter.

A man living down the road has also seen the cowled figure late at night in the same spot.

Ruins of the Carthusian priory of Hinton Charterhouse are nearby, and the habit of the Carthusians is white.

★   ★

In 1968 a woman walking near Snuff Mills, Bristol, saw the ghost of a small girl aged about eight. The little girl appeared by the river on two occasions and was accompanied by the fainter figure of another child. It was impossible to tell whether this second apparition was that of a boy or girl.

★   ★

At Kingsdown, near Bath, in Longsplatt Lane, the ghost of a child is seen running in terror when the moon is full.

★   ★

The mother of a friend of Mrs. Royal's was looking for a house in Bath before the last war and was taken by an agent to see a property in Mount Beacon. The agent stayed in the car while his client went into the house. She didn't remain there long. As soon as she entered the hall she was overcome by a feeling of horror and rushed out into

6

the road. The agent then told her that a man had hanged himself in the hall.

The house was later bought by friends, but the wife would never stay there on her own.

★   ★

A man walks straight through the walls of the rectory at Cold Ashton.

★   ★

At Gaudy Farm, Wooley, near Bradford-on-Avon, a phantom drummer is heard every so often on the anniversary of the Battle of Lansdown which took place in the Civil War.

The story is that a drummer boy was brought to the farm after the battle and died upstairs.

★   ★

A headless man walks up Perrymead, just off Prior Park Road, Bath.

★   ★

A Mr. Sebastian Cliffe was driving his car along the Warminster Road out of Bath and was approaching a bend near the Limpley Stoke viaduct, when he saw the gauges on his dashboard were not working and felt a sudden chill.

As he continued round the bend a face appeared outside his windscreen and then slowly faded. The gauges sprang back to life.

★   ★

Mrs. Thale who became Mrs. Piozzi, lived in No. 8 Gay Street, Bath, in the eighteenth century. The house has a haunted drawing-room. Voices are heard conversing, but if the door is opened, they cease.

We are told that Mrs. Thale frequently entertained Dr. Johnson to a dish of tea. Can it be their conversation that is heard?

There are other haunted houses in Gay Street. One farther up on the left, was requisitioned by the American military police during the last war. This house had something that so unnerved them that they disliked being there alone.

★   ★

A doctor visiting an ancient house in Cold Ashton, near Bath, was talking to his young patient's father in a downstairs passage which

7

runs right through the house, back to the front. A man suddenly walked right through, and out of the front door. "Who's that?" asked our doctor friend. "We've no idea," said the owner. "He often appears, and we're quite used to him."

★   ★

The wooded road leading down to Avoncliff, near Bradford-on-Avon, is haunted by the ghost of a woman. The story is that she was a witch who met with her coven in the woods above. It is believed that she walks down the road to drown herself in the Avon below.

The Man in the Black Hat (*Bath*)

The apparition of a man in a black hat and old-fashioned cloak who is seen in Saville Row, Bennett Street, and Russell Street – all near Bath's Assembly Rooms – is well documented.

The four sketches printed here were all made independently by four different eye witnesses who are complete strangers to each other.

The best description of the man (who still continues to be seen) was carried by the *Bath Evening Chronicle* on March 16, 1950.

Mrs. Cynthia Montefiore told the Chronicle: "I was walking from Portland Place to George Street. When I reached the end of Saville Row a man approached me from the corner of Evans and Owens store.

"He wore a large black hat, rather resembling the old-fashioned Quaker hat. His coat, which was also black, was cut in the pattern of the eighteenth century – threequarter length and full-skirted. From the calf down he appeared to be wearing breeches.

"He crossed the road noiselessly and came abreast of me as I gained the end of Saville Row. There was no-one else in sight. And then I suddenly had the feeling that the person I was facing was odd and unearthly. I had that peculiar sinking feeling in the stomach but I definitely did not feel frightened. I am much too interested in the occult to be afraid.

"As he passed I turned around. I turned immediately. I just had to. I wanted to see his back. But he had vanished completely.

"He certainly had no time to enter a doorway, as not two seconds had elapsed from the time he passed until I looked back. I had a distinct view of him. He was small, thin and walked with a stoop."

Another person who saw the man in the black hat was a Mrs.

Eileen Parish of Alderley, Wotton-under-Edge, Gloucestershire, who wrote to the authors in October, 1974.

"I thought I would let you know that I also have seen the Man in the Black Hat in Saville Row", wrote Mrs. Parrish.

The four sketches of the Man in the Black Hat shown here were all made in 1972 by people who have seen the apparition. They are: (1) of the man seen in Saville Row by Mrs. Harrison of Gordon Road, Bath; (2) of the man seen in Bennett Street by Mrs. Jill Dixon of Twerton; (3) seen by W.E.G. of Kensington, Bath, again in Bennett Street, and (4) by Mrs. Cynthia Montefiore as related in the accompanying story.

"It was early this year, about May, I think. I was trying to park my car opposite Evans and Owens and he came down Saville Row, stepped into the road, hesitated, turned back and began to walk towards the front of the Assembly Rooms.

"I took my eyes off him for a moment and when I looked again he had vanished, although he could not *possibly* have got to the end of the road.

"He was dressed very much like Guy Fawkes and, as he turned, his black cloak swirled out around him. He seemed to have black breeches and gaiters on. I must admit that I never thought of him as being a ghost, which is strange as I have had many ghostly experiences in Africa where I normally live and can always tell if a place is haunted.

"I also write ghost stories (fiction)."

A Mr. Emmett, who had been a regimental sergeant-major, and was for many years caretaker at the Assembly Rooms, also saw this ghost. One day he was stoking the boiler in the boiler room when he sensed he was being watched. He turned, and in the doorway stood a figure in a cloak and black hat.

As he stared, astonished, the man disappeared.

On another occasion, a woman who was watching a film crew at work near the Assembly Rooms noticed an oddly dressed man standing beside her. She was most upset when he suddenly vanished.

Lord Howe Lingers On (*Bath*)

The ghost of Admiral Howe, created First Lord of the Admiralty in 1783, and commander of the Channel Fleet in the French War when it won 'the glorious first of June' victory off Ushant in 1794, haunts No. 71 Pulteney Street, Bath. Mrs. Sheila Haines, who used to occupy a basement flat in the building, saw his lordship on several occasions and was 'frightened out of her life'.

Mrs. Haines' husband was, at that time, a policeman and had to leave the house at four a.m. One morning, about ten minutes after he had left, she heard footsteps outside in the passage. "The bedroom door opened and in came this man in naval uniform. I was lying in bed. The door opened and he just walked in. He had a look round. I was speechless. I heard the bedroom door shut, he walked back down the passage and that was it. He was quite pleasant and behaved as if he were checking the place. I saw him three or four times. It was just as though he were an ordinary living person.

"There was a noise with this manifestation. On one morning in particular it was just as though somebody had come in soaking wet. The passageway was stone and as he got outside the bedroom door I could tell by the noise what he was doing. He took his hat off and shook it and then I heard him take his boots off. He had a job with his boots and he puffed and he blew. He came into the bedroom with his boots in his hand, walked across to a recessed cupboard, into it and disappeared."

Two years ago Mrs. Haines went back to the house next door, to No. 71 Pulteney Street. The woman then living there said she had seen a man in naval uniform come out of a wall in the house. She had not known of Mrs. Haines' experience.

Is that you Ebenezer Ash? (*Bath*)

One of the most persistent and regular of Bath's ghosts used to tap at exactly 10.30 a.m. every Thursday in the Registry of Births and Deaths, Charles Street.

The registrar, Mr. John Deakin, first heard the tapping when he started working in the building ten years ago. He says it had been happening for some time before he came.

"At first we thought it was somebody next door chopping wood but the next building is separated from us by an alleyway. Apart from that, the sound seemed to come from downstairs where, at one time, the basement was used as a rest room for old people. The tapping used to occur three or four times and apparently came from inside the wall. It went on every Thursday for easily ten years, between ten and twelve in the morning."

People downstairs also heard the tapping, which stopped when the welfare department moved out of the building.

For several years a room just along the passage from Mr. Deakin's office was used as a waiting room. Once his colleague, Mr. Field, heard the door open and then a cough. After a few seconds he got up, looked into the room, only to find it empty. This happened on other occasions.

Another time he heard the waiting-room door open once and then open again. Mr. Field quickly went out of the front door and into the street but there was no-one in sight.

The old registers record the death in 1888 of one, Ebenezer Ash, who lived in the building when it was a bank. Mr. Ash was a porter and one night, when making his usual rounds, he clambered over some chairs, fell and died a week later in a coma.

Horror on the A4 (*Corsham*)

A Mr. Laurie Newman, at that time a lorry driver, of Bath, was driving from Chippenham to Bath along the A4 at 2.30 in the morning. Just before he reached Corsham he caught a figure in his headlights which was walking along the road in front of him. From the dress, he thought the person was a nun. He slowed down and pulled out a little. Just before he reached the figure it turned and he saw a white blur where the face was. Suddenly it sprang and, catching hold of the cab of the lorry, hung on and stared through the glass of the side window at him. To his complete horror he saw, instead of a normal human face, a grinning skull!

The apparition continued to cling on to the cab for a few moments and then vanished.

Mr. Newman was so shocked and upset by this nightmarish experience that he was unable to talk about it for three months afterwards. Eventually, however, he met a woman when delivering goods to London Airport who was psychic. He told her about the experience and she reassured him that he would never see the fleshless phantom again. To his intense relief, he never has.

The Case of the Remorseful Retainer (*Bath*)

This story about York Villa, Bath, was related to Margaret Royal by a friend who came to live in the house in 1910. The house in its earlier years had been occupied for sometime by Frederick, Duke of York, second son of George III. The Duke had a number of mistresses, one of whom, plus their two children, he kept at York Villa.

One day he decided to break off the relationship and go back to London. His mistress decided to follow him and instructed the staff – in particular an old family retainer – to look after the children while she went off to keep an eye on the Duke.

Unfortunately, neither the retainer nor the staff had been paid, so they left the house and the two children starved to death. The retainer did, however, return and was filled with remorse when he found the children dead as a result of his neglect. It is his ghost that is supposed to have haunted York Villa over the years. The haunting takes the form of footsteps which move up the stairs and then stop.

During the last war somebody who was staying in the house came downstairs and asked, "Who is that I saw in a long cloak and long trousers? It doesn't look as if he belongs to the house; I met him on the stairs as I was coming down this morning."

There have also been very fleeting sightings of a woman in grey. Mrs. Royal's informant says she saw her once going up into a big room a the top of the house and that her brother is supposed to have seen the spectre of a young boy when he himself was very young.

The building is now a Social Club belonging to Bath Bus Co.

Strange Happenings in Two Bristol Pubs (*Bristol*)

When Mrs. Valerie Watson and her husband used to run the 'White Hart' in Lower Maudlin Street, Bristol (from May, 1972–June, 1974) they were woken at night by things being thrown about in the bedroom while in the kitchen some unseen hand moved cups about the place, sometimes two or three times an hour. Bread rolls would be sent flying off the table.

In the bedroom, Mrs. Watson watched a pair of shoes jumping from one spot to another and back again.

The pub is 300 years old and the poltergeist is thought to be that of a monk or a victim of the plague. It would be very active for three or four weeks and would then stop. It was not without a sense of humour. A workman once tried to shift a beam in the pub, using a 28lb. sledge hammer, but was unable to do so. When he turned his back, the beam hit him on the back of the head. He retaliated with the sledge hammer but was again unable to make any impression on the beam.

When Jim Tonkin, formerly landlord of the 'New Inn', Backwell, near Bristol, first moved there, he and his wife heard footsteps coming upstairs to their bedroom. Mr. Tonkin went to see who was making the noise but couldn't find anybody.

On another occasion a ghostly stranger suddenly appeared in the middle of the night sitting on a bar stool and in the same bar a

13

woman was touched on the neck by another, non-existent, customer. Mrs. Tonkin's spectacles disappeared from the bar and reappeared in the skittle alley. The 'pineapple' top of an ice bucket was once gently wafted across the room.

The Haunted Inn (*Glastonbury*)

The 'George and Pilgrim' Hotel, Glastonbury, was built as an inn in 1475 by Abbot Selwood to provide board and lodging for those pilgrims to Glastonbury who could afford to pay for their keep. This is why the front of the hotel looks very much like a church.

The proprietor of the hotel is Jack Richardson who has been there for about ten years. The hotel, he says, has a haunted room.

"I haven't experienced it myself but I have spoken to a woman guest who has. She was staying in the haunted room and saw the ghost of a monk which appeared with two other forms that didn't quite materialise but remained in a sort of vapour.

"The monk himself was very, very clear indeed and the story is that a monk did, in fact, commit suicide in that room which is called the haunted cell.

"It's a twin-bedded room and this woman was very definite about what she had seen. She said that when he arrived he was talking about Queen Elizabeth and then he sat on her bed. She thought it was very strange because I understand you can't normally feel ghosts. She, however, could feel the sheets and blankets being pulled tightly across the bed.

"The apparition was fully dressed in a brown monk's habit. She didn't feel any fear but was quite delighted. He was there for probably about ten or fifteen minutes and then just faded away. The two shapes were with him the whole time but remained in the background.

"Several times", says Mr. Richardson, "our labrador has been sitting in the back bar late at night when her hackles have risen and she has stared straight across the room and has growled and barked. There was no question of somebody walking down the passage so there must be some sort of feeling about the place".

A Canadian visitor to this country who stopped deliberately at the George and Pilgrim to see whether it lived up to its haunted reputation was not disappointed.

In March, 1976 she wrote to Mrs. Royal with the following

account of her experiences when she stayed in the hotel.

"My husband and I spent a delightful holiday in England during September last year", relates Mrs. H. E. McCormack, of Winnipeg, Manitoba.

"Before leaving Canada we read an article in the Canadian *Financial Post* about Glastonbury which mentioned the haunted George and Pilgrim.

"We had never heard of an haunted hotel before and therefore decided that Glastonbury and the hotel would be a 'must' on our itinerary. We checked into room 7 on Sunday, September 14 and, after a pleasant dinner, ended the evening with a nightcap in the bar discussing the legend of Glastonbury with delightful local people.

"It was midnight when we turned in. We were unable to get the room with the four-poster bed (it had been reserved well in advance and our room had single beds).

"I was awake for a long time thinking about the haunted aspect of this hotel. Eventually, I did drop off to sleep and dreamt of being back home, spending an evening with my sisters.

"I was awakened by the sound of three footsteps and when I looked up I saw at the end of the bed my husband was sleeping in, a bright, arched, glimmering light. Within this shimmering frame, the form of a man emerged – tall, slender and grinning at me.

"He was wearing a teal-blue sports jacket, the style worn by elderly Englishmen on Sunday picnics.

"I was sure that I was still dreaming and that if I deliberately closed my eyes and opened them again, this apparition would disappear but to my astonishment this figure, surrounded by light, remained, arms at his side, still grinning.

"With this I threw back my covers and leapt into bed beside my husband. The instant he awoke, the figure vanished. I was much too frightened to turn on a light and check the time but I would guess that this adventure took place at approximately 3.00 a.m.

"We moved on to Porlock Weir the next day and I have wondered if my friend would have shown himself again had we stayed at the inn another night".

Five years later the George and Pilgrim was to provide Mrs. Royal and another foreign visitor with a further supernatural experience.

On June 12, 1980 Mrs. Royal, acting as an escort for the British Tourist Authority, met Dr. Peter Grimm and his wife, Sylvia, from Zurich and took them on a tour of Glastonbury. They were to spend that night at the George and Pilgrim.

"Dr. Grimm had never had a psychic experience but was anxious

15

to hear about them and, if possible, to have one himself ", relates Mrs. Royal.

"He and his wife were booked into Abbot Bere's Chamber where a lot of people had experienced things. We dined early and, being tired, went to bed. My room was the Nun's Cell, at the other end of the passage to the Bere Chamber. The room was very comfortable and pleasant.

"I woke up at dawn. There was a thing on the wall called the nun's prayer and as I looked at it I heard women's voices. They were not very loud – say, half a dozen women talking softly – and I couldn't understand what they were saying.

"I then got up and sat on the edge of the bed. There was then no sound of any voices.

"I was first down at breakfast and was joined by the Grimms. I asked Peter Grimm how he had slept and he replied that Sylvia had slept very well but that he had had 'a most dreadful night'.

"He told me that at times he had felt terribly cold but, worst of all, had felt himself being lifted up and then pressed down into the bed", said Mrs. Royal.

Mrs. Royal then told him about the voices and it appeared that he had had precisely the same experience. The voices, however, had lasted only a short time and had occurred earlier than Mrs. Royal's, in the hours of darkness before dawn.

Mrs. Royal has since heard from Dr. Grimm who wrote to tell her that he had had a radio in his case at the time and wondered if that had been the source of the voices. Mrs. Royal thinks this unlikely because if the radio had been on for ten minutes he would have heard more than six women talking and, in any case, it would have been impossible for her to have heard the radio from her room at the other end of the passage.

Bunty of the Beehive (*Bath*)

Another of Bath's haunted inns is the Bee Hive in Lansdown Road. The former landlord and landlady were aware of a female 'presence' for over ten years.

Their ghost frequented only the ground floor and occupied its time mainly by opening and shutting the doors to the bar, the passages and the lavatory.

Both Mr. and Mrs. Clark were very fond of their ghost whom they called 'Bunty'.

16

One day Mrs. Clark's mother was sitting watching television when she saw the lid of the laundry bin rise in the air and lower itself into place.

Bunty was obviously interested in cooking because the Clarks used to see lids of saucepans on the stove in the kitchen lifted and lowered by an unseen hand as if somebody was peering inside. Their dog, which apparently saw something they couldn't, would follow her around the room with his eyes.

Both the Clarks saw Bunty. She appeared first to Mrs. Clark and then to her husband.

They said she was a tiny woman of about fifty with short, grey curls. She wore a mop cap, a grey dress with a white apron and very shiny black button-up shoes.

The present landlord, a Mr. Kesteven, has not seen Bunty but he has heard footsteps on the stairs.

The Phantom Piper of Sydney Place (*Bath*)

A lady. who prefers to be known simply as 'Miss Alma', moved into Sydney Place, Bath, in 1939. The building is divided into flats. Since living there, Miss Alma has heard, and has been told by various other residents, of various supra-normal happenings.

When she first became a resident she told the landlady she had been woken up by somebody tapping on the door.

"The landlady asked me, 'Did it sound like this – one, one-two-three, one?' and she tapped on the side of my bed," said Alma. "I said, yes, that was the sound, and she said: 'There's a spirit not at rest here; I was going to get the rector to come over but I never did'.

"One night I was in bed and someone seemed to catch hold of me and tried to pull me out of bed. That really did frighten me; in fact, it made me cry with fright."

Later, she saw the outline of a human figure on a stool by her bed. Her brother saw the same figure, in the same place. He said it was that of a man.

At the end of 1974, Miss Alma again saw the shape of the man by the side of her bed. "This time he had bagpipes over his shoulder but before I could ask him to play me a tune he was gone," she said.

Phantom shapes have also been seen on the stairs of Sydney Place, including a white figure. There have also been footsteps. Other residents have heard furniture being moved about.

The Fatal Pint (*Norton St. Philip*)

A customer who stopped for a pint at the 'Fleur de Lys' public house, Norton St. Philip, near Bath, nearly 300 years ago paid for it with his life. His spirit still lingers on in the pub.

The famous 'George Inn', opposite the 'Fleur', was then being used as a court house where those who had taken part in the Duke of Monmouth's unsuccessful rebellion were being tried for their lives. Several had been sentenced to be hanged. The place of execution was an orchard behind the 'Fleur de Lys'. As the batch of condemned men was being led through a passage in the pub, the unfortunate customer held a gate open for them, was mistaken for one of the rebels and was executed with the rest.

Mr. William Harris, who became landlord of the 'Fleur de Lys' in October, 1974, says that the office in the pub is said to be haunted by the ghost of the innocent victim.

"Since I've been here, I've neither seen nor 'felt' a ghost but you do hear the most peculiar noises. For instance, on two or three occasions when I've been up in the lounge I've suddenly heard what I thought was our dog coming up the passage. He has a chain round his neck and it jangles. I've leapt up and have opened the door, only to find that there's nobody there. The dog has been lying at my feet all the time."

His wife was ironing in a small room off the passage when she saw a shadowy figure go past the open door up the passage when the pub was closed and empty. On two occasions, their dog has refused to go into the office.

The previous landlords also had a dog. One day they left it for an hour or so, locked in the office. When they returned and let the animal out it bolted, apparently terrified, and was run over and killed in the road outside the pub.

People comment on the icy cold of the passage.

Wordsworth's Lady? (*Bath*)

The 'Grosvenor Hotel', Bath, has been haunted for a number of years. The house at one time belonged to Wordsworth, the poet.

On the first floor, at the top of the stairs to the left across the corridor, there is a door. One morning, at about 2.30 a.m. Beverly Bush, the son of the manageress, had climbed the stairs and was about to enter his mother's flat when he heard footsteps on the other side of the door in the corridor.

When he opened the door to investigate he saw the grey, misty figure of a woman and at the same time felt an icy chill. He followed the figure as it turned right into the conference room. When he got there, however, the room was empty but a chair at one of the long tables was pulled back by an unseen hand and an ashtray on the table was lifted and replaced.

Beverly left in a hurry.

A friend of the family, a Mr. Gordon Hall, had a similar experience to Beverly's at 2.45 p.m. one Christmas Day. Mr. Hall was carrying a tray of coffee up to the flat when he, too, heard footsteps coming from behind the same door. He put the tray down, wrenched the door open and immediately felt the same icy chill. The misty figure rushed past him into the corridor.

Molly, who helps at the 'Grosvenor', was in the second floor corridor when she saw the figure of a woman leave a room, quickly cross the corridor and, presumably, go down the stairs opposite.

Molly says the woman was dressed in grey and she thought at first it was a colleague but the girl was later found to have been nowhere near the corridor at the time. In any event, the colour of her hair was different.

The Terrified Diner (*Bath*)

Next door to Bath's Theatre Royal is Beau Nash's house. Here he lived with his last mistress, Juliana Popjoy.

It is said that after his death Juliana vowed never to sleep in a bed again, and became a herb gatherer in Wiltshire, living in a hollow tree.

Richard and Juliana's ghosts have been seen upstairs. Though not recently it seems. But, has Juliana's? ·

Just before Christmas 1975, a traveller arriving too late for a meal in the hotel where he had booked, was recommended to Popjoy's Restaurant, which Beau Nash's house is now called. Ordering his meal, he went upstairs to the big room which was once the drawing room of the house, to have an aperitif while his meal was being prepared. He sat down on a green settee. A lady came and sat down beside him and then – promptly vanished!

Terrified, the man rushed down the stairs, gave a brief explanation to the people there, and dashed into the street.

The Lady in Grey? (*Bath*)

Like the Garrick's Head pub, Bath's Theatre Royal, which is next door, is enlivened by the occasional appearance of the Grey Lady.

A stagehand called Tim told Mrs. Royal that he was helping set the stage for an amateur production when he looked up and saw the Grey Lady in the circle. She was walking, not *along* the rows of seats, but diagonally through them. He immediately stopped what he was doing and rushed up to the circle which when he got there was deserted. There was no sign of the Grey Lady – except what he describes as a very pleasant smell of a jasmine scented perfume.

Two girls sitting in the theatre's upper circle have seen the woman's ghost sitting in a box. She was wearing white lace gloves.

A friend of Mrs. Royal's, a nursing sister at one of the Bath hospitals, has also seen the Grey Lady. On this occasion the phantom was sitting in the box next to hers, watching the play. She was wearing an old-fashioned dress and was again wearing white gloves. Quite suddenly she disappeared.

The Lady in Grey was also seen in August, 1975 by the cast of the *Dame of Sark,* which included Miss Anna Neagle.

In June, 1963 a clock being used as a prop during a play that was enjoying its Bath Festival premiere started striking during the performance. The odd thing about it was that its mechanism had been removed.

Mr. Fred Sadoff, the producer, said afterwards: "It was fantastic. The hands were pointed at 12.30 but right at the big moment it chimed loudly three times. Then the lights dimmed just at the right moment without anyone touching them. Ever since then the cast has been talking about ghosts. We can't think of any other explanation".

The Nun of Larkhall Place (*Bath*)

Mrs. Christine Mead of 15 Larkhall Place, Bath, was in her kitchen one day when she heard somebody calling. She turned round, looked into the living-room and saw a black figure, very much like a nun. The figure was still there a few moments later. It was just over five feet tall, stockily built and there was a blur where her face should have been.

On other occasions, Mrs. Mead has been upstairs when she has heard somebody call her name. The house has always proved to be empty.

The apparition, which remains visible for about five minutes, appears at about the time Mrs. Mead's father died and is accompanied by a musty smell in the hall. She says she feels no fear of the ghost but looks on it as a guardian.

The room where it appears is long and contains at one end the kitchen, divided off by glass doors opening into the lounge. The opposite end is well-lighted by windows.

Another strange occurrence: before the house was modernised the toothbrushes were always kept in a cupboard. When somebody went to get them they would always have been moved to a different place.

The Story of Sally (*Bath/Bradford-on-Avon*)

Sally-in-the-Wood is a well-known area on the road between Bath and Bradford-on-Avon.

Its fame or notoriety rests nowadays on the frequency with which vehicles plunge off the road at that particular spot. But its other claim to fame is that it is haunted by the ghost of Sally, an old gipsy woman, from whom it takes its name.

A television engineer told Mrs. Royal that he was driving through the area when his girl friend suddenly shouted to him that there was a woman crossing the road in front of him. He saw nothing.

Other people have had a similar experience.

The Black Figure (*Bath*)

Stephen and Diane Forcey returned home to their first floor flat in No. 17 Broad Street, Bath, at 11 p.m. after an evening with Diane's mother. The date was November 29th, 1974.

The house which contains the flat is 300 years old and is owned by Diane's father.

That evening Stephen and Diane had climbed the steep stairs and had opened the front door of their flat. Entering the sitting room, they noticed that it was 'unusually quiet'. There was 'a different feeling'. This made them stop and listen and from the kitchen they heard a distinct 'chink' as if a tumbler had been struck.

Stephen went forward immediately into the kitchen and looked around. He glanced through the doorway on the right that opens on to a landing that has a flight of stairs leading down to their bathroom. The stairs used to lead to the shop below.

Stephen saw a tall, black figure moving along the landing. It ducked its head as if to look at the first step and disappeared down the stairs.

The figure was approximately six foot tall and made no sound. Its face was not visible, being covered by some sort of cowl.

The Forcey's have since heard one sharp knock on the entrance door to their flat. This has occurred many times, day and night. When they open the door, there is no-one there.

Diane's mother says Diane's father had the shop as a newsagents. About fifteen years ago the lad employed by them went out to the back of the house to collect some papers. He returned quickly, his face ashen. He said, "I've seen a ghost," and then described the same figure that Stephen was to see in November, 1974.

Until Diane's mother told them the story, Stephen had never heard the boy's story and Diane's mother had forgotten about it until they recounted their experience.

The lad, now married with children, remembers the figure he saw clearly.

Black and White Shapes at the Royal Oak
(*Near Warminster*)

The 'Royal Oak' at Corsley Heath, near Warminster, has been a pub for many years. Originally it was run as a hospice by the Friars of Longleat and is still part of Lord Bath's estate. Legend has it that there is an underground tunnel connecting the 'Royal Oak' with Longleat, three miles away.

Mr. Gerald Whiting, the present landlord, says that several people claim to have seen apparitions in the pub, including his wife who, he says, "Is a very level headed person, who doesn't believe in ghosts.

"She will not use the staircase at the end of the house – she'll go up it but she will not come down, because she feels she's being pushed. Other people have said the same.

"Another landlord's wife saw a black shape standing at the end of her bed and my wife has seen a white shape in the kitchen about the size of the refrigerator which measures 5ft by 6ins.

"It moved across the kitchen and through the wall where the doors used to be before the house was altered."

Both Mr. Whiting and his son, Francis, have felt a presence in the pub whom they call 'Charley'.

Legend has it that 200 years ago a 12-year-old boy fell into a vat of boiling beer in the pub and was scalded to death.

The Watcher by the Bed (*Trowbridge*)

The middle bedroom of the 'George Inn', Trowbridge, has its own peculiar atmosphere. A helper, John Rose, who has slept in the room, says he has woken with a tingling sensation all over his body.

"I tried to make myself wake up but couldn't. It felt as if there was somebody standing by the side of the bed bending over me. I managed to get out of bed and walk to the door. It was only when I had closed it behind me that I managed to open my eyes properly. I have had this experience five or six times in two years and it always happens between 1.30 and 2.00 o'clock in the morning."

Supernaturally, in Avalon (*Wedmore*)

The lovely village of Wedmore stands on its own 'island', close to the southern border of Mendip, in the vale of Avalon.

Its church is dedicated to St. Mary the Virgin and is known as The Cathedral of the Moors. As Desmond Hawkins records in his book, *Avalon and Sedgemoor*, it has a compact and sturdy central tower. "In the centuries since it was built the parishioners of Wedmore have watched the sea flow past their island, inundating the low moors as far as Glastonbury, and many a local traveller must have offered more than a perfunctory prayer to St. Christopher."

Next door to the church there stands 'The George Inn', 620 years old and supposedly one of the few English inns built over a graveyard, which may account for some of the odd goings-on in 'The George'.

Betty Henderson and her husband, Don, took over the inn in 1972. The first of the family to see a ghost was the Henderson's son, Michael.

"After we'd been there for about three months," said Mrs. Henderson, "Michael got up one night and went to the bathroom which is at the end of the corridor in one of the oldest parts of the building. He was washing his hands in the basin and looking into the mirror over the basin when all of a sudden his own face was blotted out and he saw this woman standing at the side of him. She was watching him with a curious expression, as much as to say, 'Who are you'.

"My son thought, 'That's funny, who's in here with me?'. When he turned round there was nobody there. He turned round again to look in the mirror and there she was. She was dressed in an Edwardian style blouse with a high neck to it and had long black hair with a lot of grey in it. She had an elderly, kindly face. He didn't see her again.

"The next happening was at a private Christmas party held in our restaurant here. A young woman of twenty-six was staying with her family. Her mother and her little sister were staying in room No. 6 and she had to walk from room 6 to room 1, which is down the corridor in a different part of the hotel."

"As she was walking along the corridor she saw this dark figure dressed in a long black skirt, with the same sort of shirt as the apparition seen by my son. When the figure reached this girl's bedroom it passed straight through the door.

"She didn't bother to go into the bedroom but dashed back to her parents' room and slept there.

"After that nothing was seen for months until one evening in the bar. It was winter and our young barmaid, Liz, was behind the bar and there was one elderly farmer, John Duckett, standing in the corner. All of a sudden he pointed to a glass cup in a corner of the bar that was turning round and round without anybody touching it.

"Mr. Duckett turned and said, 'The little old lady's around again; she's come in for her drop of gin'.

Liz told me that just before the glass had started to move it had gone icy cold in the bar.

"Room 1 goes cold in exactly the same way. I was in there cleaning one day when all of a sudden it turned freezing and I felt as if someone was looking over my shoulder watching me. It wasn't exactly nasty but it gave me a funny feeling. I got out of the room quickly."

The 'George Inn' also has a resident incubus which the Henderson's are thinking of asking the church to do something about. The incubus is in a room at the top of the house. Three people have felt its presence – Mrs. Henderson's son, Michael; her husband, Don, and a woman staying at 'The George'.

The woman was in bed asleep one night when all of a sudden she woke up with a terrible start. Something was holding her hands tight and wouldn't let go. She struggled to get away, but it still held on. Eventually, when she had shouted at it, it released her. When she looked across the room she saw a thick white object by the washbasin. As soon as she put the light on it all disappeared and everything returned to normal.

Don Henderson, who was resting in the afternoon in the room told his wife that he was woken up by something pressing him down on the bed. "I couldn't move my arms, my legs, my head or my hands," he said. After shouting at the incubus for the best part of a quarter of an hour it released him. Michael occupied the room for some time. The only way he could get to sleep at night was by having the light on.

His experiences were similar to his father's.

Sceptics Beware! (*Monkton Farleigh*)

The 'King's Arms' inn at Monkton Farleigh, near Bath, is the scene of some quite impressive hauntings.

One winter's night, Ken Jefferson, a regular caller, was sitting to the right of the fire at about 11.00 p.m. when he and the others present in the bar heard the sound of a large bird flying noisily across the room. From the sound, the bird seemed to fly from the bar, right down the room and straight through the wall at the opposite end.

The noise of the bird's flight seemed to come from four feet above the ground. Mr. Jefferson's description is of 'a large pigeon taking off' and he says he felt an icy chill as it went by. The bird has been heard at least a dozen times on various occasions.

Just after the present managers, Eric and Nancy Muspratt, came to the 'King's Head' in September, 1973, Eric returned home at 1.30 a.m. but could not sleep. The house was silent. Suddenly he heard the door which opens on to the stairs from the bar creak slowly open.

He heard footsteps coming up the stairs and go along the passage. The footsteps seemed to be of heavy boots on stone (the floor is wooden) and they continued along the passage as far as the bathroom door, paused and then returned the way they had come.

Mr. Muspratt, who had been motionless with surprise, leapt out of bed and rushed down stairs. Everything was as normal.

Earlier in the evening his wife had been entertaining some friends, one of whom had also heard heavy footsteps coming from upstairs.

The 'King's Arms' phantom apparently does not like people to say that there are no such things as ghosts.

In 1974 a customer's expression of disbelief was immediately followed by a loud crash from upstairs and water started pouring through the ceiling. A freezer that Mr. Muspratt had been defrosting had turned a complete somersault and was lying on its face.

On another occasion a tray of steaks was hurled across the preparation room following a similar remark.

Christine, the waitress at the inn, says that when her mother knew the inn forty years ago it was known to be haunted. In the room behind the band platform an old woman has been heard talking to children.

Then there is the strange story of the ancient key which was discovered recently when part of a wall was being demolished to make a doorway to give access to the restaurant. It is a large key, pitted with age.

During the demolition two small, aged countrymen arrived in the bar, only to declare, "No good will come of knocking down that wall!"

The two had never been seen before and have never been seen since. Curiously enough, after their visit the phenomena became more active.

The 'King's Arms' was originally a Cluniac house founded in 1120 and re-built in the early 13th century. It was dedicated to St. Mary Magdalene and is supposed to have had a girdle belonging to her donated by the Empress Maud.

A Fiery Haunt (*Bristol*)

According to a report in the *Western Daily Press*, Bristol, in October, 1975, a ghost is supposed to haunt the Avon fire brigade's new £1,200,000 headquarters in Temple Back, Bristol.

It has been seen no less than nine times.

The apparition, which walks through doors, lowers the temperature in centrally-heated rooms and vanishes into thin air, appears only at night.

A cook, Mrs. Iris Rhodes, has seen it three times. "I was standing counting my money at about 8.30 p.m. when I saw someone standing by the pillar," she told a reporter.

"As I went towards him, he disappeared."

On another occasion, she chased him downstairs with a glass of water.

"I thought someone was playing a joke on me, but he had vanished," she said. "A person could not have got through the locked doors at the bottom of the stairs."

The ghost looked as if it was between thirty and thirty-six and was wearing a large mackintosh. "He had ruddy cheeks, looked ever so healthy and was of medium height," said Mrs. Rhodes.

Some firemen who have seen the ghost says he was wearing mediaeval dress. One theory is that it could be the ghost of one of the Knights Templar, a crusading and banking order, which owned the area from 1140 until 1308, when they were arrested for heresy and blasphemy.

The Vanishing Trick (*Tockington/Rudgeway*)

This strange story concerns a brother and sister, a Mr. and Miss Cooper, who some years ago were walking along a lane between Tockington and Rudgeway, some five miles from Thornbury.

It was twilight and the lane ran between hedges roughly four feet high. Glancing over the hedge to their right they saw a man on horseback about thirty feet away in the field. He was riding a big chestnut and was wearing a high hat and a black cloak.

The man was travelling diagonally across the field towards a gate in the hedge where they expected him to make his exit. They could have taken their eyes off the man for no more than a couple of seconds to look at the gate but when they looked back into the field, which was large and flat, both horse and rider had vanished.

The Thrifty Phantom (*Bath*)

Years ago, reported the *Bath and West Evening Chronicle* in 1975, a man who lived and died in Milsom Street, Bath, ran his own 'save it' campaign, switching off lights and closing doors.

"The trouble is he is still doing it," said the newspaper.

When the door started to bang, Mr. Richard Lever, manager at South West Rentals in Milsom Street, wasn't worried. He put it down to the old building.

Then the light in one room went off with no one near and a television set in the showroom started changing channels by itself.

Mr. Lever was baffled. "I don't say I believe in ghosts but some force here is doing something," he said at the time.

One morning the television changed channels twice.

"It isn't a control that you can set off by radio; it's a push-button control and it takes a lot of force to press it. Yet the programmes changed," he said.

Once Mr. Lever was in an old kitchen on the second floor when the light went off.

"The switch was down when I went in and up when I went out. I was so scared the hairs rose at the back of my neck and I dropped a cup."

The switch was checked by an electrician who found there was nothing wrong with it.

On the same floor a door closes when there is no draught and no one about. Above, there is a room that neither Mr. Lever nor his assistant, Mr. Grenville Chard, will willingly enter.

"There is just something about it that says you don't need to go in," said Mr. Chard.

Exactly the same phenomena occurred when the premises were a boutique.

"There was a man called Walker who owned this place years ago and died here," said Mr. Lever. "He had a mania for closing doors and switching lights off – just what is going on now."

Mr. Lever has been told that the room at the top of the building that neither he nor his assistant like entering might have been the old man's flat or office.

"If it is Mr. Walker, he has apparently been around for years and done no harm," said Mr. Lever, "My smoking has increased, though."

The Phantom Hiker (*Nunnery/Critchill*)

Motorists travelling between the villages of Nunney and Critchill, near Frome, should think twice before they pick up hitch-hikers late at night for it could be the phantom hiker of Nunney.

Three motorists travelling in the area late at night have reported picking up a stranger who has asked them to take him to Nunney Catch. He wears a check sports jacket and is between thirty and forty.

On each occasion the man has climbed into the car but on arrival at Nunney Catch has disappeared.

Frome police report that one man was so frightened by the occurrence that he reported the matter to them.

Another was so shocked that he had to have hospital treatment.

Why a Family Fled in Terror (*Twerton*)

A sensational haunting made headlines in the Bath and Bristol newspapers in May, 1975.

The victims were a Mr. John Oliver, his wife, Doreen and their five children, Karen, Deborah, Kim, Darren and Kai, who were eventually forced to leave their council home in Cameley Green, Twerton.

On three successive nights Mrs. Oliver was approached by a ghost-like being, an old man with a 'horrible wrinkled skin." The first time she saw it she thought it had been a nightmare. The second time, according to a report in the *Bath and West Evening Chronicle*, she fainted. When her husband woke up she was fighting with the sheets.

Mrs. Oliver said, "It was a big black thing which didn't seem to have a face."

On the third occasion, the couple were sharing their bed with their youngest child, Kai, and a 17-year-old, Patrina Hart, who lived with the family. Patrina was feeding Kai in the early hours of the morning when she suddenly felt she was being watched.

"I turned to look at Mrs. Oliver, and she was staring at me," said Patrina. "She was asleep but her eyes were all white and the expression on her face frightened me to death."

"Then she started groaning and her body began to vibrate from head to foot. She didn't stop until we turned the light on."

After that experience the Olivers left the house but were persuaded to return for one night. By 2.30 a.m. they had again left in a hurry after seeing a picture swing from side to side 'like a windscreen wiper', hearing strange noises and feeling icy blasts of air.

Another victim of the haunting, Mr. Oliver's then brother-in-law to be, Mr. David Saul, was so badly frightened he had to have psychiatric treatment.

Mr. Oliver subsequently told a newspaper reporter: "I don't care whether you believe it or not; we've been through it. That thing was trying to possess my wife."

Bath City Council remained unmoved by the reports, but finally agreed to re-house the Olivers in another council house in Cranmore Place, Bath.

"It was necessary on medical and social grounds to move the household from this property," said Mr. Adrian Britton, of the city's estates department.

"We accept that the tenant is convinced about the ghost but that should not be taken to mean that we accept that the house is haunted."

Shortly after the Olivers had left the house for the second time a reporter from the *Western Daily Press* spent a night there alone with a copy of *The Exorcist* by William Peter Blatty for company. His account was headed 'My vigil with the spooks of Cameley Green . . .'.

However, the night was uneventful. "As far as I am concerned there is no spook in the Cameley Green house," wrote John Roulston.

The house was re-let shortly afterwards and there have been no further reports of ghostly happenings up to the time of writing.

Tragedy and Murder in York Street (*Bath*)

A number of macabre and interesting stories are attached to No. 13 York Street, Bath. They were related to Mrs. Royal by a Miss Dorothy Melluish.

Miss Melluish's one-time fiancée, Mr. Arthur Wiseman, lived in the house as a child. Some years before the Wiseman family moved in a young boy had apparently been scalded to death in the kitchen. A bath had been prepared in front of the kitchen range. Tragically, the child, who had been playing, fell into the near-boiling water.

The Wisemans often heard the sound of a ball being bounced on the stairs leading from the ground floor down to the passage that runs past the kitchen. There was also the ghostly figure of a woman in white whom they saw hurrying down the passage, passing through a doorway and vanishing through arches set into the wall beyond.

The house itself is built on part of the monastery that was attached to Bath Abbey. The arches in the basement area were part of the site of the monastery graveyard. Bones were found when flagstones were lifted in this part of the house.

At one time No. 13 was left untenanted after the brutal murder of a woman who, Mr. Wiseman told Miss Melluish, was killed upstairs. Her corpse was dragged downstairs by the murderer who then packed it in a trunk. He was discovered when the trunk burst open as he was loading it into a cab.

The Spectre at No. 3 (*Bath*)

The basement flat of No. 3, The Circus, Bath, is reputedly haunted by the ghost of a woman in a long grey dress.

In the late 1950's and early 60's the flat became the home of a Miss E. W. who has since left Bath. When the workmen were decorating the flat before she moved in none of them liked to be alone on the premises even though the work was undertaken during the day because the men said the flat was haunted.

When Miss E. W. took up residence things began to happen which puzzled her. For instance, when certain objects such as books and magazines were placed by her tidily on the centre table of the room (the writer of this report knew Miss E. W. intimately and was often in her flat) she would find they had been moved to other parts of the room. Being in no way alarmed by these happenings, she took the trouble to draw outlines in chalk around certain objects, to check on the phenomena. Very often she found the objects either inches away from the chalk lines or in a totally different place from where she had left them.

The writer of this report was once having tea in the flat on a hot summer's afternoon without a vestige of a breeze. Suddenly, a large maidenhair fern started to sway from side to side as if moved by a strong wind. She pointed this out to her hostess who said this sort of thing was constantly happening, and that when she was in bed, with the lights out, she often heard someone moving quietly around the room, but never saw anything. Her cleaning woman, on the other hand, declared that she often saw the figure of a woman in a long dress, sitting by the fireside, but was always too scared to address it.

There was a communicating door between the sitting-room and the dining-room. A figure was seen to rush past this door, when it was open, but when a search was made nothing living was to be seen.

The entire house once belonged to a titled man, whose coat of arms is still to be seen in the hallway. It is said, although there is nothing to prove it, that Miss E. W.'s flat, which was once the servants' quarters (in those days when there was a certain nobility attached to the art of 'service') and that the figure to be seen rushing through, was the ghost of one of the serving women, running from the unwelcome advances of a man-servant.